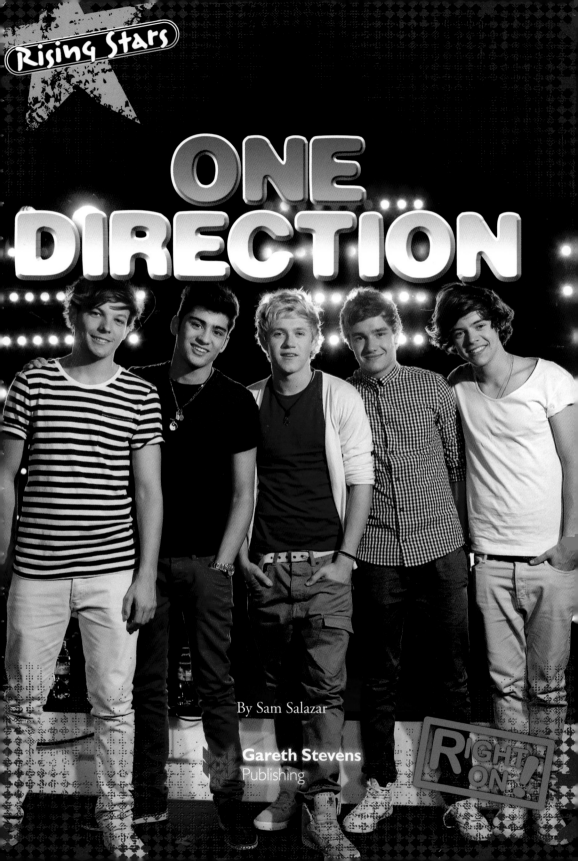

Rising Stars

ONE DIRECTION

By Sam Salazar

Gareth Stevens
Publishing

Right ON!

Please visit our website, www.garethstevens.com. For a free color catalog of all our high-quality books, call toll free 1-800-542-2595 or fax 1-877-542-2596.

Library of Congress Cataloging-in-Publication Data

Salazar, Sam.
One Direction / by Sam Salazar.
  p. cm. — (Rising stars)
Includes index.
ISBN 978-1-4339-8986-5 (pbk.)
ISBN 978-1-4339-8987-2 (6-pack)
ISBN 978-1-4339-8985-8 (library binding)
1. One Direction (Musical group) — Juvenile literature. 2. Rock musicians — England — Biography — Juvenile literature. 3. Boy bands — England — Juvenile literature. I. Title.
ML3930.O66 S25 2014
921—d23

First Edition

Published in 2014 by Gareth Stevens Publishing
111 East 14th Street, Suite 349
New York, NY 10003

Designer: Nick Domiano
Editor: Therese Shea

Photo credits: Cover, p. 1 Newspix/Newspix/Getty Images; pp. 5, 17 Stephen Lovekin/Getty Images Entertainment/Getty Images; p. 7 KENZO TRIBOUILLARD/AFP/Getty Images; p. 9 FOX/Getty Images Entertainment/Getty Images; p. 11 Gareth Cattermole/Getty Images Entertainment/Getty Images; p. 13 Christopher Polk/Getty Images Entertainment/Getty Images; p. 15 Hagen Hopkins/Getty Images Entertainment/Getty Images; p. 17 Stephen Lovekin/Getty Images Entertainment/Getty Images; pp. 19, 23 Kevin Mazur/WireImage/Getty Images; p. 21 Danny Martindale/WireImage/Getty Images; p. 25 Slaven Vlasic/Getty Images Entertainment/Getty Images; p. 27 Juan Naharro/Getty Images Entertainment/Getty Images; p. 29 TIZIANA FABI/AFP/Getty Images.

Printed in the United States of America

CPSIA compliance information: Batch #CS13GS: For further information contact Gareth Stevens, New York, New York at 1-800-542-2595.

Contents

Five Guys, One Group

One Direction is one of the biggest bands in the world. The five members are Liam Payne, Louis Tomlinson, Niall Horan, Harry Styles, and Zayn Malik.

Beginnings

The members of the band got their start on the British TV show *The X Factor*. They all started out as solo artists in 2010.

Each singer almost got voted off!

The judges thought they should

have another chance. They put them

together as a group.

The members of One Direction are all close in age. They became good friends and learned to sing together.

Still Winners

One Direction won third place on *The X Factor*. However, many people thought they were the best act. They wanted to hear more.

13

In 2011, One Direction released their first song, "What Makes You Beautiful." It went to the top of the music charts.

Meet the Group

Niall Horan is the only Irish member of the band. He wants to be the Irish Justin Bieber! He plays the guitar.

Harry Styles was in a band called White Eskimo in school. He was the lead singer. He also worked in a bakery!

Liam Payne tried out for *The X Factor* in 2008. The judges told him to come back when he was older. Two years later, he got a standing ovation!

21

Louis Tomlinson acted in TV shows before he was on *The X Factor*. He was also in musicals at his school.

23

Zayn Malik's real first name is Zain.

He changed it for *The X Factor*.

Zayn almost left the show because he

couldn't dance!

Albums

In 2012, One Direction put out their first album. It was called *Up All Night*. They toured the world.

One Direction's next album was *Take Me Home*. They were named MTV's Artist of the Year in 2012. What's next for this young group?

Timeline

1991   Louis Tomlinson is born December 24.

1993   Zayn Malik is born January 12.

1993   Liam Payne is born August 29.

1993   Niall Horan is born September 13.

1994   Harry Styles is born February 1.

2010   Each member tries out for *The X Factor*.

2011   The band releases "What Makes You Beautiful."

2012   The band releases *Up All Night* and *Take Me Home*.

2012   The band is named MTV's Artist of the Year.

Books

Linker, David, ed. *One Direction: A Year with One Direction.*
New York, NY: HarperCollins, 2013.

Mattern, Joanne. *One Direction.* Hockessin, DE:
Mitchell Lane, 2013.

Peppas, Lynn. *One Direction.* New York, NY:
Crabtree Publishing, 2013.

Websites

One Direction

www.mtv.com/artists/one-direction/
Watch videos and see photos of the band.

One Direction

www.onedirectionmusic.com/us/home/
Find out what the boys are up to on their official website.

Publisher's note to educators and parents: Our editors have carefully reviewed these websites to ensure that they are suitable for students. Many websites change frequently, however, and we cannot guarantee that a site's future contents will continue to meet our high standards of quality and educational value. Be advised that students should be closely supervised whenever they access the Internet.

Glossary

release: to make something ready for use or sale

solo artist: someone who sings or plays music alone

standing ovation: when a crowd stands to clap for someone's actions

tour: to go to many places in order to play and sing music for people

Index